Standing In The Need of Prayer

Project preview

Published by FastPencil Publishing

First Edition

http://fp.fastpencil.com

Printed in the United States of America

Table of Contents

PRAYER

Sometimes do you ever think of prayer to be something difficult? Well in reality it is not what your mind think of it as it is simply what it means it is "prayer". We all know that our heavenly Father will respond to our prayers with power and grace and reign down on the just as well as the unjust.God hears everyone's prayer and he knows what we are going to pray before we begin to pray. To simply understand what pray is you have understand that prayer is simply a way to deepen your relationship with God. In attempt to express our soul's deepest longings to God leaves us silent state. Jesus knew his followers would struggle as they attempted to talk with God. In the Lord's Prayer, Jesus gave us an illustration *how* to pray. Rather than just reciting his words we can learn from Jesus himself. Every prayer that Jesus prayed included worship,thanksgiving, a declaration of faith, confession of sin,and petition . Our Lord's example can help us put everything in words what our long to say to God. Do you need a boost in your prayer life? Then you will love these resources on prayer. They will help you deepen your own communion with the Lord. Remember that God loves you, and his ear is inclined in you direction. Sometimes our prayer life needs a jolt out of the rut it has fallen into. We tend to use the same phrases over and over again. We tend to default to worn out phrases or words. We fall in the patterns of mindless repetition. The devil hates prayer. Our own flesh does not naturally love it.Therefore, it does not come full-born and complete and passionate from the womb of our hearts. It takes renewing our mind and spirit daily and it takes self-discipline.The power of prayer should not be underestimated. James 5:16-18 declares, "...The prayer of a righteous man is powerful and effective. Elijah was a man just like us. He prayed earnestly that it would not rain, and it did not rain on the land for three and a half years. Again he prayed, and the heavens gave rain, and the earth produced its crops." God most definitely listens to prayers, answers prayers, and moves in response to prayers.

Jesus taught, "...I tell you the truth, if you have faith as small as a mustard seed, you can say to this mountain, 'Move from here to there' and it will move. Nothing will be impossible for you" (Matthew 17:20). 2 Corinthians 10:4-5 tells us, "The weapons we fight with are not the weapons of the world. On the contrary, **they have divine power** to demolish strongholds. We demolish arguments and every pretension that sets itself up against the knowledge of God, and we take captive every thought to make it obedient to Christ." The Bible urges us, "And pray in the Spirit on all occasions with all kinds of prayers and requests.

With this in mind, be alert and always keep on praying for all the saints" (Ephesians 6:18).

Power Of Prayer - How do I tap into it?
The power of prayer is not the result of the person praying. Rather, the power resides in the God who is being prayed to. 1 John 5:14-15 tells us, "This is the confidence we have in approaching God: that if we ask anything according to his will, he hears us. And if we know that he hears us - whatever we ask - we know that we have what we asked of him." No matter the person praying, the passion behind the prayer, or the purpose of the prayer - God answers prayers that are in agreement with His will. His answers are not always yes, but are always in our best interest. When our desires line up with His will, we will come to understand that in time. When we pray passionately and purposefully, according to God's will, God responds powerfully!

We cannot access powerful prayer by using "magic formulas." Our prayers being answered is not based on the eloquence of our prayers. We don't have to use certain words or phrases to get God to answer our prayers. In fact, Jesus rebukes those who pray using repetitions, "And when you pray, do not keep on babbling like pagans, for they think they will be heard because of their many words. Do not be like them, for your Father knows what you need before you ask him" (Matthew 6:7-8). Prayer is communicating with God. All you have to do is ask God for His help. Psalm 107:28-30reminds us, "Then they cried out to the LORD in their trouble, and he brought them out of their distress. He stilled the storm to a whisper; the waves of the sea were hushed. They were glad when it grew calm, and he guided them to their desired haven." There is power in prayer!

Power Of Prayer - For what kind of things should I pray?

God's help through the power of prayer is available for all kinds of requests and issues. Philippians 4:6-7 tells us, "Do not be anxious about anything, but in everything, by prayer and petition, with thanksgiving, **present your requests to God.** And the peace of God, which transcends all understanding, will guard your hearts and your minds in Christ Jesus." If you need an example of a prayer, read Matthew 6:9-13. These verses are known as the Lord's prayer. The Lord's prayer is not a prayer we are supposed to memorize and simply recite to God. It is only an example of how to pray and the things that should go into a prayer - worship, trust in God, requests, confession, protection, etc. Pray for these kinds of things, but speak to God using your own words.

The Word of God is full of accounts describing the power of prayer in various situations. The power of prayer has overcome enemies (Psalm 6:9-10), conquered death (2 Kings 4:3-36), brought healing (James 5:14-15), and defeated demons (Mark 9:29). God, through prayer, opens eyes, changes hearts, heals wounds, and grants wisdom (James 1:5). The power of prayer should never be underestimated because it draws on the glory and might of the infinitely powerful God of the universe! Daniel 4:35 proclaims,

"All the peoples of the earth are regarded as nothing. He does as he pleases with the powers of heaven and the peoples of the earth. No one can hold back his hand or say to him: We have all sinned and deserve God's judgment. God, the Father, sent His only Son to satisfy that judgment for those who believe in Him. Jesus, the creator and eternal Son of God, who lived a sinless life, loves us so much that He died for our sins, taking the punishment that we deserve, was buried, and rose from the dead according to the Bible. If you truly believe and trust this in your heart, receiving Jesus alone as your Savior, declaring, "Jesus is Lord," you will be saved from judgement and spend eternity with God in heaven. As we pray, and consecrate ourselves before God we need to remember that God hears our prayer. He listen to our prayer as so as we begin to start speaking.

DRAFT

When I Pray

Growing up as a child I always thought that prayer was only what people did before meals or when they were faced with difficult trials. I would pray before meals and, occasionally, I would pray if I was struggling with something that I couldn't control, and I would do all of these things, without understanding why I felt the need to pray.

Last year as I began to grow in my relationship with God I began to learn about the real significance of prayer. I learned that prayer is not a ritual it is a way of communication and a way of expressing ourselves to God and deepen our relationship with him. God wants to have a relationship with us and get to know us like we his own. It is true that He knows what is in our hearts and minds because God is all knowing, and God wants us to tell these things that are important to us to him. God tells us to call upon him and he wants us to ask him questions, He wants us to seek him with all our hearts, and He wants us to knock so that doors can be opened for us. When we doing these things we get the best gift of all, which is to know God personally and to have a relationship with him.

Through prayer, God grows us in our understanding of him. He shows us how deeply he cares for us and helps us to understand how powerful He truly is. This past year I have had the opportunity to attend several prayer meetings and have even been blessed with the opportunity to lead prayer meetings this semester as well. In doing so, every time we meet with God to pray, I am blown away by the bold prayers that students use to cry out to God. I've come to realize that we can humble ourselves before Him and pray such bold, impossible prayers because God is infinitely powerful and nothing we pray is too small for Him.

As Christians, we tend to downplay prayer, often seeing it as the last thing to do rather than the first. In an attempt to encourage one another, we tell each other, "Just pray about it." We gravely underestimate prayer, its significance, and its power, and, in so doing, we are robbed of the joy that God intended for us to experience through prayer.

It is through prayer that I talk to God, and because I love talking to Him and I love growing in my relationship with Him, I find myself trying to encourage other people to do the same. I want people to experience the joy and love that is intended for us in knowing Him through prayers. It is through faith in God that we are able to receive the blessings of God.**Jesus set forth clear, precise, and specific rules governing the practice of prayer. We find them in the Sermon on the Mount and, contrasting with some commandments of the Sermon, these rules are easy to obey. Yet the churchmen in general ig-**

nore them just as they do the hard commandments. This practice of disobedience, of both the hard and the easy commandments, can only result when people don't really care about Jesus and his commandments. They do not love Jesus, for if they did, even a little bit, they would surely obey the easy ones! Jesus had other things to say that are relevant here and I direct you first to two utterances: If you love me, you will keep my commandments. (John 14:15) Why do you call me 'Lord, Lord,' and not do what I tell you? (Luke 6:46)**This prime commandment applies not only to prayer but also to almsgiving and fasting, and to any other practice that can be defined as "piety." The thing is, when we pray publicly, we are seen by others. And, it is unarguable that, with some exceptions, we do it to be seen by the others. Otherwise, why do people not obey the rules of our Lord and pray only in secret, in obedience to his command? We should also note that this general rule is also a very easy one to keep.Very important now to note that Jesus was not praying while presenting the model prayer, hereafter referred to as "the Prayer". He was addressing the disciples with instructions on prayer. He was not addressing the Father and so was not violating these three rules. He clearly intended the disciples to obey all the rules by taking the Prayer back to their rooms, closing the door, and praying to the Father in secret. They surely obeyed them, for there is no evidence in the New Testament that they ever had the practice (of the modern church) of uttering this prayer in unison in their gatherings. That would**

break the secrecy rule!Jesus submitted brief and simple rules of piety, including the practice of prayer. The rules require that one enter into one's room, close the door, and pray in secret. Then he immediately followed, as part of the same text, with a model prayer that the churchmen have made a public ritual!

Let us ask some simple questions: Is it reasonable to expect the Father to hear and respond positively to communications directed to him in violation of his established protocol? Is it reasonable to believe that they love Jesus who consistently ignore protocol and violate his commandments after this manner? Is it reasonable to think that the Father accepts worship that consists of an act of gross insubordination?

I do not need here to present an answer to these questions. You will know, in your hearts, what is the only reasonable answer!

God Hears You

God hears your prayer and he knew what you needed even before you asked him. He delights when we come to him and ask him to help us. God wants to give us the things we need, not the things we think we need. Sometimes the answers we get to prayers aren't what we want or expect. They sometimes take longer than we think they should. But, none of that is the absence of answers. God hears ever prayer no matter what method of praying you use whether it is speaking, singing, or thinking. Even our actions can be a prayer to God. God's word says "The eyes of the Lord are on the righteous and his ears are attentive to their cry ". God never sleeps and always available to hear our prayer. We must humble ourselves and seek Him.We are told that God answered the prayers of the people because they trusted in Him. Believing that God will answer our prayers, trusting in his ability to hear and answer is very important. Many places in the Bible have similar conditions for prayers to be heard. Living right, trusting in God, and being humble is really what you need for God to do anything for you. In other words, the prayers that are heard are those that come from a person who has a relationship with God, someone who believes that his or her prayers will be answered by a loving Heavenly Father. We learned earlier that God talks to us in the Bible. In prayer, you are talking with God. He knows you better and loves you more than any friend. He wants to spend time with you and hear from you.No, God does not answer the prayers of Christians who are in sin. When we say they are "in sin," we are saying that they are abiding in it and not repenting of their sin. God says he will not hear their prayers.Psalm 66:18, "If I regard wickedness in my heart, the Lord will not hear."Proverbs 1:28-29, "Then they will call on me, but I will not answer; They will seek me diligently, but they shall not find me, 29 Because they hated knowledge, And did not choose the fear of the Lord.

We can see from Psalm 66:18 that if we as believers are to "regard wickedness" in our hearts, then the Lord will not hear our prayers. In other words, he won't answer them. However, when we pray for forgiveness and we are repentant, God, of course, hears and forgives. But what does it mean to regard wickedness in your heart? The literal translation is "see iniquity with pleasure." So, if anyone, Christian included, were to look upon sin favorably and seek to do it, then God will not hear their prayers. Sin hinders prayer's effectiveness, and as we see in the next verse, Isaiah 59:2, God hides himself from those who are in sin. In James 4:3 we see that wrong motives hinder prayer.

Proverbs 1:28-29 tells us that God will not answer those who hate his knowledge and do not fear him. Anyone, Christian included, who would willfully abide in sin is not choosing the fear of the Lord. Therefore, God will not listen to him and his prayers will be hindered.The prayer of repentance and forgiveness is heard.

If you're a Christian who is abiding in sin, then what you need to do is pray to the Lord and confess your sin and then repent of it and be cleansed. God will forgive, and your fellowship with him will be restored.

- 1 John 1:9, "If we confess our sins, He is faithful and righteous to forgive us our sins and to cleanse us from all unrighteousness."

You need to trust in Christ and what he has done. You need to realize that all of our sins are cleansed in Jesus. But, if you continue to abide in sin, then God will not answer your prayers.God wants you to bring your concerns to Him. Yet two things can keep Him from giving you what you ask for: sin–going against His will, or asking for something that goes against His will.

God knows what's best for you, but because sin separates you from Him, you must turn to His Son, Jesus Christ, who paid the price for your sins. When you do, the barrier is removed and God hears your prayers.Are youready for a real relationship with Christ? Only He provides a direct connection to God and brings you peace.

DRAFT

Watch and Pray

The apostles in the bible exhort us to actively "watch"! We need to understand all that they meant and the wide-ranging implications. Our survival and salvation could depend on that understanding and action!

The apostle Paul wrote to the Christians in Corinth, “Watch, stand fast in the faith, be brave, be strong” . The rest of the verse is clear, but what does “watch” mean?

Paul wasn’t telling us to be passive spectators—of entertainment or anything else. He meant something far different.

It is spiritual watching coupled with prayer that gives one the strength to survive temptations and difficult situations.

This article focuses on New Testament scriptures with the verb “watch”—important scriptures that are often misunderstood, ignored and neglected.

How important is it that we “watch”? Consider this: The biblical command to watch is several times coupled with the command to pray. Is prayer important? Extremely so! And so is the command to watch!

Watch means to stay wide awake

When the New Testament commands us to "watch," it is usually the translation of one of two Greek words (Gregorio and arguendo), which have similar meanings–to "stay awake" and to "be sleepless." They are usually meant in the metaphorical and spiritual sense–to be vigilant and on guard, fully awake, aware, alert and intently focused–with several applications and implications.

In Matthew 26:37-40, the meaning of "watch" is primarily physical. Jesus was chiding the disciples for not remaining awake during the hour preceding His arrest.

But what Jesus next said to Peter had a deeper, spiritual meaning: "Watch and pray, lest you enter into temptation. The spirit indeed is willing [i.e., intentions are good], but the flesh [mere human willpower] is weak' " (Matthew 26:41).

It is spiritual watching coupled with prayer that gives one the strength to survive temptations and difficult situations.

"Awake to righteousness, and do not sin" (1 Corinthians 15:34). Being awake is equated with righteousness and not sinning. Paul was writing to the church at Corinth, which shows that even true Christians can be spiritually asleep to varying degrees.

Paul also wrote: "And do this, knowing the time, that now it is high time to awake out of sleep; for now our salvation is nearer than when we first believed" (Romans 13:11, emphasis added throughout).

In other words, the closer we draw to the second coming of Christ, the more urgent it is that we awake out of spiritual sleep! Indeed, we have entered the fearful end-time years that are the grand climax of human civilization. If ever there was a time to pay attention and get prepared, it is now!

Furthermore, none of us knows when he or she will die. Being spiritually prepared for the end of life should be our top priority.

Watching means properly using our minds

God gave us marvelous minds to use —to study, learn, observe, analyze, judge and think.

Life is time. To waste time is to waste life. Many people are mentally lazy—wasting a tragic amount of time on the trivial and temporal, mundane and materialistic. Many squander countless hours vegetating in front of their TV or computer seeking only to be entertained.

Real readers are becoming rare. A society becomes shallow and superficial when most citizens rely too much on pictures

and images rather than words. In-depth learning requires language.

It is quite significant that God's true religion is based on spoken and written messages that were compiled into what we call the Bible. God's people are to be "people of the Book." In contrast, most pagan religions emphasize images, idols, symbols and rituals.

You see, God wants His people to zealously read and study, to think and meditate. He wants us to be well-informed regarding the major geopolitical, cultural and spiritual issues and events of our time. God deplores ignorance, indifference and being "dull of hearing" (Hebrews 5:11).

This is where the Bible comes in, providing the essential framework for a godly worldview. The Bible is God's divine revelation of absolute truth, which is just as relevant today as it ever was.

Because of this, the Bible should be the prism, lens and filter by which we can accurately perceive and judge all other information. It enables us to develop a godly worldview—the framework and foundation by which we can accurately interpret all that is going on in the world. We can then understand our confusing world scene with amazing clarity, sense and logic!

Jesus rebuked the Pharisees and Sadducees for their hard-hearted mind-set. If they had not had evil attitudes and had believed the Scriptures, they would have been able to "discern the signs of the times" and to realize the Messiah had come (Matthew 16:1-3).

We need knowledge of end-time prophecy

To know where to focus our attention, we particularly need to know the Bible prophecies of the end time, especially the prophecies surrounding the second coming of Christ.

We are to "eagerly wait for" Christ's return, not just passively wait around (Hebrews 9:28). Jesus was emphatic that His followers should hope for His return, expect His return and pray for His return! In addition, our enthusiastic anticipation and excitement will intensify as we see more and more world events fulfilling Bible prophecies—especially those that point to the increasing nearness of Christ's return.

Note the watching, waiting, anticipation and preparedness in the following passage:

"Let your waist be girded and your lamps burning; and you yourselves be like men who wait for their master, when he will return from the wedding, that when he comes and knocks they may open to him immediately. Blessed are those servants whom the master when he comes, will find watching ".

Jesus concluded His message by saying, "Therefore you also be ready, for the Son of Man is coming at an hour you do not expect".

Much later, Jesus echoed that point: "Behold, I am coming as a thief [meaning suddenly and unexpectedly]. Blessed is he who watches, and keeps his garments, lest he walk naked and they see his shame". Wearing garments, especially white raiment, symbolizes a good spiritual condition . We must not be caught undressed–unprepared.

Christ's all-important end-time prophecy

Jesus gave a crucial end-time prophecy shortly before His crucifixion, recorded in Matthew 24, Mark 13 and Luke 21. It's valuable to study this prophecy often.

Jesus' disciples wanted to know what to watch for. "Tell us, when will these things be? And what will be the sign of Your coming, and of the end of the age?" (Matthew 24:3).

Significantly, the very first thing that Jesus responded with was a somber warning of what to watch out for: "Take heed that no one deceives you" (Matthew 24:4). Sadly, many are deceived. Many who call themselves Christians are deceived into thinking that Christ will not literally return to the earth, even though He repeatedly promised He would, or that He will return in some manner different from what He told us.

In the rest of the chapter, Jesus answers their questions by revealing the future key trends and conditions for which it would be critically important to watch.

Jesus then urged His disciples to "watch therefore, for you do not know what hour your Lord is coming. But know this, that if the master of the house had known what hour the thief would come, he would have watched and not allowed his house to be broken into" (Matthew 24:42-43).

After Jesus' resurrection, He again said, "It is not for you to know times or seasons which the Father has put in His own authority" (Acts 1:7). However, in spite of Jesus' statements, countless people have foolishly tried to predict the time of His second coming. It is because we don't know the timing that we must keep watching.

Continuing in Matthew 24, Jesus said, "Therefore you also be ready, for the Son of Man is coming at an hour you do not expect" (Matthew 24:44) Watching reminds us and motivates us to remain ready. That's the main idea!

Shortly after, Jesus warns of the temptation to think, "My master is staying away a long time" (Matthew 24:48, New International Version). When a person thinks he has more than enough time to get ready, he is seriously tempted to let down spiritually (Matthew 24:49-51).

The parable of the 10 virgins (Matthew 25:1-13) emphasizes staying spiritually prepared and ready. Keeping one's lamp filled with oil represents staying close to God and staying filled with the Holy Spirit. Jesus concluded the parable by saying, "Watch therefore, for you know neither the day nor the hour in which the Son of Man is coming" (March 25:13).

Watching, praying, staying sober and watching out for enemies

In Mark's and Luke's accounts of Jesus Christ's prophecy, we see that Jesus connected watching with praying. There is much to pray about regarding the present and the future. Watching helps our praying, and praying helps our watching.

Mark records Jesus saying: "Take heed, watch and pray; for you do not know when the time [of Christ's coming] is. It is like a man going to a far country, who left his house and gave authority to his servants, and to each his work, and commanded the doorkeeper to watch" (Mark 13:33-34; see also verses Mark 13:35-37).

So also remember when you pray watch and be prayful of your surroundings because the devil loves to try to interfer with your prayer.

DRAFT

Prayer and the Difference It Makes

Throughout the Bible, believers are called to pray. But what is prayer? What does it mean to "pray without ceasing?" And does prayer really make a difference? Before delving too deeply into the topic of prayer, it will be beneficial to first define the term, as well as the focus of our prayers–God.

Prayer and God's Nature

Let's start with the second part. In order to develop a clear idea of prayer, we must first have a clear idea of God. Biblically speaking, God is a personal being. This is critical to prayer because it means that God is a person we can interact with, that He has a will and that we are able to relate to Him on a meaningful level. If He were impersonal, then prayer would not be meaningful. If He were personal, but uncaring and distant, prayer wouldn't serve a purpose.

Not only is God personal, He is also loving (1 John 4:8, 16; John 3:16). This is also important in relation to prayer. If God were personal, but uncaring or unkind, then prayer might do us more harm than good! But God is not only loving, He is all loving (omnibenevolent). In relation to prayer, this means that God always desires the best for us because He loves us.

God is also all-powerful (omnipotent), meaning that no prayer is beyond His ability to answer, "For nothing is impossible with God" (Luke 1:37). If God were less than all powerful, then we would have no assurance that He could answer or even hear our prayers.

The fact that God is all-knowing (omniscient) is also significant to the concept of prayer. If God were limited, then He would not know all that is happening in His creation. If this were the case, He might overlook our prayers because they might be beyond His knowledge. Fortunately, the Bible is clear that God knows everything (see, for instance, Psalm 139:2-4; 147: 4-5; Isaiah 46:10). In relation to God's omniscience, Jesus said, "Your Father knows what you need before you ask him" (Matthew 6:8).

God is also wise and holy. He knows what is best for us, as well as what will lead us to holiness rather than sin. He is also immanent, meaning that God is active in His creation in a personal way, not only directing greater matters of history but also involved in the life of everyone. This means that no prayer is too great for Him, but also that no prayer is too small for Him.

While we cannot explore all of God's attributes here, one final one to note, of utmost importance to prayer is God's sovereignty. God is supremely in charge of everything that happens in His universe. Nothing takes Him by surprise and nothing happens in our lives without the knowledge of God, even though we may not always understand His actions: "'For my thoughts are not your thoughts, neither are your ways my ways,' declares the LORD. 'As the heavens are higher than the earth, so are my ways higher than your ways and my thoughts than your thoughts'" (Isaiah 55:8-9).

In hearing and responding to our prayers, then, we are assured that God will do so on the basis of His many attributes. His personal nature, love, power, knowledge, wisdom, holiness, immanence and sovereignty all play a role in how we relate to God in prayer and how He relates to us.

What Prayer Is Not

Now that we have a clearer understanding of God's nature, it may be tempting to delve right into a definition of prayer. But first let's take a brief look at what prayer is not (this is by no means an exhaustive list):

Prayer is not magic. We cannot summon God as though He were a genie, waiting to grant our wishes without regard for our circumstances or the consequences.

Prayer does not make demands. While we can make requests of God in prayer, we dare not make demands. God is the Creator of the universe and does not take orders from us.

Prayer is for our benefit, not God's. We need a relationship with God, available to us through Jesus Christ and engaged primarily through prayer because we were made to function best when we are in a proper relationship with our Creator.

Prayer is not a guarantee against suffering. "In this world, you will have trouble" (John 16:33); "Dear friends, do not be surprised at the painful trial you are suffering, as though something strange was happening to you. But rejoice that you participate in the sufferings of Christ, so that you may be overjoyed when his glory is revealed" (1 Peter 4:12-13).

Prayer is not an opportunity for us to show off. "And when you pray, do not be like the hypocrites, for they love to pray standing in the synagogues and on the street corners to be see by men.

In addition, our attitude in prayer is important. We must not be haughty, but humble. Seen in this light, to "pray continually" means, in one sense, that we must always strive to have a prayerful attitude. Our prayers must come often and regularly, not from legalistic duty, but from a humble heart, realizing our dependence on God in every aspect of our lives. As we journey together in understanding the nature and purpose of prayer, it is my prayer that God will bless these words and instill a joyful and fruitful prayer life in your life and mine. Prayer can make a profound difference in our world. But it is up to us to offer our prayers humbly and regularly.

The Availability of Prayer

Prayer Has No Barriers

In short, prayer has no barriers. Governments cannot stop it, our location cannot stop it and enemies in the spiritual realm cannot stop it.

As noted earlier, "Prayer is an open door which none can shut." But there is one way to shut it and that is when we choose disbelief over belief. Our own anxieties can stop the power of prayer if we allow them to stifle the truth that prayer is always available to us. God is always ready to listen, no matter what our circumstances, but we must speak to Him in prayer.

In reference to the power of evangelism, the Apostle Paul wrote, "'Everyone who calls on the name of the Lord will be saved.' How, then, can they call on the one they have not believed in? And how can they believe in the one of whom they have not heard? And how can they hear without someone preaching to them? And how can they preach unless they are sent? As it is written, 'How beautiful are the feet of those who bring good news!'". Similarly, when we pray to God we will be heard. But how can God hear unless we pray? How can our prayers be received unless they are sent? How beautiful are the prayers of those who seek the Lord, despite their circumstances?

Prayer is always available to us, but far too often we turn to God in prayer as a last resort, not a first response.

God Wants to Hear Our Prayers

Is God too busy to hear our prayers? Is He occupied with weightier matters than our lives and troubles? Unlike the worldview of deism, which claims that God created and wound up the universe like a watchmaker winds a watch, leaving it to run on its own, God really cares not only about the larger scheme of the universe, but also for each person. He is not a deaf god like the god of deism, but a caring and active God. He transcends His creation but is immanent–or active–in it. No prayer is too small for God to hear. Neither is any prayer too large for God to handle.

As Christ said, "Look at the birds of the air; they do not sow or reap or store away in barns, and yet your heavenly Father feeds them. Are you not much more valuable than they?" The answer to the question asked by Jesus is that we are indeed "more valuable than they," for we are created in God's image "we are God's workmanship, and He loves us.

An important step in receiving the blessings of prayer is to humbly and sincerely offer our prayers to God. Fortunately, we can do this anywhere and anytime, because prayer is always available to us. But we must take the initiative. If we do so, God is eager to hear us, comfort us, strengthen us, help us, and uphold us with His "righteous right hand".

DRAFT

Prayer Has Its Reason

One key reason to pray is that God has commanded us to pray. If we are to be obedient to His will, then prayer must be part of our life in Him. A prayer is an act of obedience. God calls us to pray and we must respond. Why did Jesus pray? One reason he prayed was as an example so that we could learn from him. Prayer allows us to worship and praise the Lord. It also allows us to offer a confession of our sins, which should lead to our genuine repentance. Moreover, prayer grants us the opportunity to present our requests to God. All of these aspects of prayer involve communication with our Creator. He is personal, cares for us, and wants to commune with us through prayer. Prayer is not just about asking for God's blessings – though we are welcome to do so – it is about communication with the living God. Without communication, relationships fall apart. So, too, our relationship with God suffers when we do not communicate with Him. Does God need our help? No. He is all powerful and in control of everything in His creation. Why do we need to pray? Because prayer is the means God has ordained for some things to happen. Prayer, for instance, helps others know the love of Jesus. Prayer can clear human obstacles out of the way in order for God to work. It is not that God can't work without our prayers, but that He has established prayer as part of His plan for accomplishing His will in this world. Can physical strength help us overcome obstacles and challenges in the spiritual realm? No, "For our struggle is not against flesh and blood, but against the rulers, against the authorities, against the powers of this dark world and against the spiritual forces of evil in the heavenly realms. But in prayer, even the physically weak can become strong in the spiritual realm. As such, we can call upon God to grant us power over evil. This point is covered separately in another article. But, in short, another reason to pray is that prayer is always available to us. Nothing can keep us from approaching God in prayer except our own choices. Humility is a virtue God desires in us.

Learning from the Prayer Life of Jesus

Jesus prayed for others. In Matthew 19:13, we read, "Then little children were brought to Jesus for him to place his hands on them and pray for them." Despite *the fact that "the disciples rebuked those who brought them,"* Jesus said *the children should not be hindered "for the kingdom of heaven belongs to such as these.* In John 17:9 *we read,* "I [Jesus] *pray for them.* I *am not praying for the world, but for those you have given* Me, *for they are* Yours." This *underscores the need for intercessory prayer.*

Jesus *prayed with others.*Luke 9:28 *reads,* "[Jesus] *took* Peter, *John and James with* Him *and went up onto a mountain to pray."* Jesus *prayed alone, as we'll read below, but* He *also knew the value of praying with others.* Acts 1:14 *underscores the importance of* Christians *praying with one another:* "They *all joined together constantly in prayer.*

Jesus *prayed alone.*Luke 5:16 *reads,* "But Jesus *often withdrew to lonely places and prayed."* As *much as* Jesus *understood the value of praying with and for others,* He *also understood the need to pray alone.* Psalm 46:10 *reads,* "Be *still, and know that* I *am* God." Some-

times it's important for us to "be still" before God, but the only way to do this, especially in our hectic culture, is to do so alone with God.

Jesus prayed in nature. Psalm 19:1 reads, "The heavens declare the glory of God; the skies proclaim the work of his hands." What better place to commune with our Creator than among the wonders of nature? Luke 6:12 says, "One of those days Jesus went out to a mountainside to pray ..." He could have gone to a home, a synagogue or if He were near Jerusalem he could have gone to the temple to pray. But there were times when Jesus made the decision to pray where He was, which often happened to be in nature. We are surrounded by so much that is "man made" that sometimes it's difficult for us to remember that this is not our world, but God's world full of wonders for us to enjoy.

PROBING THE PROBLEMS OF PRAYER

Most of us have encountered problems in our prayer lives to one degree or another. Maybe God did not answer our prayer. Or we encountered a moral dilemma such as should we pray for or against enemies? Perhaps we wonder whether or not prayer is worth bothering about. After all, if everything is already going to happen according to God's will, then our prayers cannot possible change His mind, right? While space will not allow us to go into detail on matters relating to problems and prayer, in this article we will try to probe the issues biblically and reasonably .Do our enemies deserve our prayers? The answer to this problem of prayer is easy and hard. It is easy, biblically speaking, because Christ said, "You have heard that it was said, 'Love your neighbor and hate your enemy.' But I tell you: Love your enemies and pray for those who persecute you. But this directive to love and pray for our enemies is a problem for us sometimes because our natural inclination is not to pray for our enemies. But by seeking to imitate Christ, we grow in our level of maturity enabling us to love and pray for our enemies.But doesn't the Bible support praying *against* our enemies? There are instances in the Psalms, for instance, where prayers openly ask God to defeat enemies. Biblically, we can pray for victory over enemies, but coupled with the command to love our enemies, we should not do so spitefully or out of malice. We should pray for the defeat of enemies with the right attitude – that of wanting to see God's Kingdom increase, not to satisfy our petty grudges. God is just, but He is also merciful. Therefore, praying for God's justice to prevail against enemies is right. We should also keep in mind that there are instances where our enemies are not truly fellow human beings, but "the spiritual forces of evil in the heavenly realms. What if two people are praying for opposite results? Does God just flip a coin and decide to answer the prayer of one person, but not another? No, God is not arbitrary. In fact, if prayers are in opposition He may decide not to answer either one. But it's also possible He will answer the prayer of one person, but not the other. Why? This is a question we don't always have the answer to. We usually only see a fraction of the tapestry that God is weaving throughout history and in our lives. This is not easy for us to understand, particularly when our prayer happens to be the one that has seemingly gone unanswered, but we can be assured that God's will has not been thwarted. He simply has other plans for us and, therefore, we must trust Him to always do what is in our best interest in the long term. Does God only hear the prayers of Christians? Or of faithful Christians? What about people of other faiths? Will God hear their prayers, too? Will He answer them? The theological answer to the question is that yes, God, being all knowing, must hear everyone's prayers. So He does hear the prayers of Christians and non-Christians alike. But hearing and answering are different matters. If God were to answer the prayer of someone involved in a false religious system, we can surmise that God would do so only if His answer would lead them closer to truth rather than closer to error. Also, there may be instances where an adherent of another religion – or even a Christian – might attribute something to God answering prayer, but that may not necessarily be the case. It may be that a series of circumstances have resulted in what we believe to be an answer to prayer when in reality it was not. This, of course, is difficult if not impossible to determine and should not lead us to doubt God's hand at work in our lives. However, assuming the seeming answer to prayer is not against God's clearly revealed will, and assuming that the apparent answer leads us closer to truth and closer to God, then there is no real reason to doubt God's involvement in our lives.

What Prayer Is and Isn't

Prayer is not some mystical process whereby we call out to some force. Nor is it a kind of power with which we create things or speak them into existence, ordering God around like some bell-hop who art in Heaven. Prayer is communicating with and hearing from God.

True prayer is what happens when our will is aligned with the will of God, and we pray accordingly. Prayer is our connection to Heaven and Heaven's connection to us—that is why you should always keep the lines open! Perhaps you used to pray when you were a small child, or you started to pray as a young Christian, but it seemed as though God always answered your prayers with a resounding "No!" Frustrated by unanswered prayer, you decided to stop praying. In doing so, you have unwittingly fallen into the sin of prayerlessness. Jesus said, "Men always ought to pray and not lose heart" (Luke 18:1). And Paul wrote that we are to "pray without ceasing. . .for this is the will of God in Christ Jesus concerning you" (1 Thessalonians 5:17–18).On the other hand, maybe you pray regularly, but your prayers never seem to get a response. It seems that all you receive is an icy silence. Perhaps you can relate to Job, who said in the midst of his trials, "Nor is there any mediator between us, who may lay his hand on us both" (Job 9:33). Job was saying that there was no one who could lay his hand upon both God and man at the same time.

But Jesus is our mediator. Being God, He knows God's desires; yet having walked on this earth as a man, He understands our weaknesses and frailties. For that reason, we can be assured that we pray to a God who does not turn a deaf ear to our prayers. Instead, He desires to communicate with us in this way.

How Should We Pray

"Praying always with all prayer and supplication in the Spirit, being watchful to this end with all perseverance and supplication for all the saints" (Ephesians 6:18). Notice the use of the word "all" in this verse. We are to pray on all occasions, with all kinds of prayer and requests, and for all the saints.

God does not teach us the posture of prayer because any posture will do.

People in the Bible prayed standing, lifting up their hands, sitting, lying down, kneeling, lifting their eyes toward Heaven, bowing, and pounding their chests.

God does not teach us the place to pray because any place will do.

Scripture tells us, "I desire therefore that the men pray everywhere" (1 Timothy 2:8). People in the Bible prayed during battle, in a cave, in a closet, in a garden, on a mountainside, by a river, by the sea, in the street, in Hades, in bed, in a home, in a prison, in the wilderness, and inside a fish.

Jesus does not tell us when to pray because any time will do.

People in the Bible are found praying early in the morning, in the mid-morning, in the evening, three times a day, before meals, after meals, at bedtime, at midnight, and day and night. People pray when they are young, when they are old, when they are in trouble, every day and always. In any posture, at any time, in any place, and under all circumstances–prayer is good and needed in the life of prayer.

What Types of Prayers We Should Pray

The Bible identifies several different types of prayers we can pray. One model for how we should pray is captured in the acronym ACTS. Each letter stands for a specific aspect of prayer, arranged in a very natural order.

A: Adoration (worship)

C: Confession (of specific sins)

T: Thanksgiving (gratitude)

S: Supplication (specific requests).

Adoration

Jesus essentially taught us the same thing in the Lord's Prayer, which begins, "Our Father which art in Heaven, hallowed be Thy name". This puts things in perspective for us. A good example of this type of adoration is found in Psalm 95:1–7. When we take the time to praise and worship God in our prayers, we are placing God where He rightfully belongs. As a result, our problems and needs come into their proper perspective.

Confession

The closer we draw to God, the more we sense our own sinfulness. When Isaiah came into God's presence, he said, "Woe is me, for I am undone!" (Isaiah 6:5). The confession of our sin removes any barriers and clears the air of anything that would cause God not to hear our prayers. "If we confess our sins, He is faithful and just to forgive us" (1 John 1:9). This is, once again, modeled in the Lord's Prayer. After "Our Father which art in Heaven," we find, "Forgive us our sins" (Matthew 6:12).

Thanksgiving

Our immediate response after confession should be Thanksgiving. We should be thankful that God would indeed cleanse and forgive us. David said, "Blessed is he whose transgression is forgiven" (Psalm 32:1).

Should we give thanks because everything is going perfectly in our lives or because we are in a good mood? No, we should give thanks because God deserves our praise. Psalm 118:1 says, "Give thanks to the Lord, for He is good! For his mercy endures forever." As another translation puts it, "His love endures forever." By giving thanks, which is simply expressing gratitude for what we have, we prevent our focus from shifting to what we do not have.

Supplication

If we are faithful in the first three steps, the last step will not degenerate into giving God our spiritual shopping list. Too often in prayer, we start with requests instead of spending time in adoration, confession, and thanksgiving first. Yet, God does want to hear our needs and requests. Scripture tells us, "Be anxious for nothing, but in everything by prayer and supplication, with thanksgiving, let your requests be made known to God" (Philippians 4:6–7).

We are also promised, "And my God shall supply all your need according to His riches in glory by Christ Jesus".

Do not neglect this vital part of your Christian walk. As someone has said, "Prayer is the breath of the newborn soul, and there can be no Christian life without it."

Abide In Christ

Jesus gave this incredible promise concerning how to have answered prayer: "If you abide in Me and My words abide in you, you will ask what you desire, and it shall be done for you" (John 15:7).

This verse can be literally translated, "If you maintain a living communion with me, and my words are at home in you, I command you to ask at once for yourselves whatever you desire. It's yours."

"Abide in Me"

If we abide in Jesus, we will automatically know God's will, and thus we will ask for it. To abide means to "maintain a living and continual fellowship with Jesus Christ." You become like two friends who are completely comfortable in each other's presence. You are not ill at ease, looking forward to getting away from that person. Instead, you enjoy being with him and you want to hear what he has to say.

This is not to say that we should be overly casual with God. As Jesus points out in His model prayer in Matthew 6:9–13, we should always begin our prayers by recognizing that we are addressing the Almighty God who is to be reverenced, worshiped and obeyed. Yet, He is also our Father in Heaven who greatly desires to hear from us and wants to be our closest and most intimate friend.

"My words abide in you"

This speaks of God's Word is at home in our hearts. Our prayers cannot be divorced from our lifestyles. They flow out of a close walk with God. If your life is not pleasing to God, your prayer life will be practically non-existent. Obedience to God certainly plays a part in answered prayers: "Whatever we ask we receive from Him because we keep His commandments and do those things that are pleasing in His sight" (1 John 3:22).

If we give a listening ear to all of God's commands to us, He will give a listening ear to all of our prayers to Him.

The Model Prayer

The disciples brought this request to Jesus after they had witnessed the countless times He went out to spend time with His Father. Likewise, this should be the heart cry of every child of God. Jesus' response to the disciples' request is found in Matthew 6:9–13:

"In this manner, therefore, pray:

'Our Father in Heaven,

Hallowed be Your name.

Your Kingdom come.

Your will be done on earth as it is in Heaven.

Give us this day our daily bread.

And forgive us our debts, as we forgive our debtors.

And do not lead us into temptation,

But deliver us from the evil one.

For Yours is the kingdom and the power and the glory forever.

Amen.

This model prayer also called "The Lord's Prayer," covers every aspect of prayer. It can be divided into two parts. The first three components of the prayer deal with God's glory: "Hallowed be Your name," "Your Kingdom come," and "Your will be done."

The second three components of the model prayer deal with our need. "Give us this day our daily bread," "Forgive us our debts," and "Lead us not into temptation." This whole prayer just breaks down the significance of the importance of how prayers is needed in all our lives.

Hinderance To Prayer

The first hindrance to prayer we will find in James 4:3, "Ye ask and receive not BECAUSE YE ASK AMISS, THAT YE MAY SPEND IT IN YOUR PLEASURES."

A selfish purpose in prayer robs prayer of power. Very many

prayers are selfish. These may be prayers for things for which it is

perfectly proper to ask, for things which it is the will of God to

give, but the motive of the prayer is entirely wrong, and so the

prayer falls powerless to the ground. [SIN] The second hindrance to prayer we find in Is. 59:1,2:"Behold, the Lord's hand is not shortened, that it cannot save;neither His ear heavy, that it cannot hear. But YOUR INIQUITIES HAVE SEPARATED BETWEEN YOU AND YOUR GOD, and YOUR SINS HAVE HID HIS FACE FROM YOU, THAT HE WILL NOT HEAR."...

Sin hinders prayer. Many a man prays and prays and prays,

and gets absolutely no answer to his prayer. Perhaps he is tempted to think that it is not the will of God to answer, or he may think

that the days when God answered prayer if He ever did, are over.3. [IDOLATRY] The third hindrance to prayer is found in Ez. 14:3, "Son of man, these men have taken their idols into their heart, and put the stumblingblock of their iniquity before their face: should I be inquired of at all by them?"(R.V.) IDOLS IN THE HEART CAUSE GOD TO REFUSE TO LISTEN TO OUR PRAYERS.

What is an idol? An idol is anything that takes the place of God, anything that is the supreme object of our affection. God alone has the right to the supreme place in our hearts. Everything and everyone else must be subordinate to Him.

The fourth hindrance to prayer is found in Prov. 21:13,"WHOSO STOPPETH HIS EARS AT THE CRY OF THE POOR, HE ALSO SHALL CRYHIMSELF, BUT SHALL NOT BE HEARD."

There is perhaps no greater hindrance to prayer than stinginess, the lack of liberality toward the poor and toward God's work. It is the one who gives generously to others who receives generously from God. The fifth hindrance to prayer is found in Mark 11:25, "And when ye stand to pray, FORGIVE, if ye have ought against any; that your Father also which is in heaven may forgive you your trespasses."

An unforgiving spirit is one of the commonest hindrances to prayer. Prayer is answered on the basis that our sins are forgiven, and God cannot deal with us on the basis of forgiveness while we are harboring ill-will against those who have wronged us. Anyone who is nursing a grudge against another has fast closed the ear of God against his own petition.

The sixth hindrance to prayer is found in 1 Peter 3:7, "Ye husbands, in like manner, dwell with your wives according to knowledge, giving honor unto the woman, as unto the weaker vessel as being also joint-heirs of the grace of life; to the end that your prayers be not hindered. Here we are plainly told that A WRONG RELATION BETWEEN HUSBAND AND WIFE IS A HINDRANCE TO PRAYER.

The seventh hindrance to prayer is found in James 1:5-7, "But if any of you lacketh wisdom, let him ask of God, who giveth to all liberally and upbraideth not; and it shall be given him. But let him ask IN FAITH, NOTHING DOUBTING: for he that doubteth is like the surge of the sea driven by the wind and tossed. For let, not that man think that he shall receive anything of the Lord."

Prayers are hindered by unbelief. God demands that we shall believe His Word absolutely. To question it is to make Him a liar.

DRAFT

PRAYER,PRAYER, AND MORE PRAYER

The love of Christ impels us,once we have come to the conviction that one died for all;
therefore, all have died.He indeed died for all,
so that those who live might no longer live for themselves
but for him who for their sake died and was raised.Consequently, from now on we regard no one according to the flesh;even if we once knew Christ according to the flesh,
yet now we know him so no longer.So whoever is in Christ is a new creation:
the old things have passed away;behold, new things have come.
And all this is from God, who has reconciled us to himself through Christ
and given us the ministry of reconciliation, namely, God was reconciling the world to himself in Christ,not counting their trespasses against them and entrusting to us the message of reconciliation.So we are ambassadors for Christ, as if God were appealing through us.

We implore you on behalf of Christ, be reconciled to God. For our sake he made him to be sin who did not know sin, so that we might become the righteousness of God in him.

Prayer Moves Mountains

Amazing, isn't it, that our prayers, whether grand and glorious or feeble and faint, can move the very heart of God who created the universe? To walk with God we must make it a practice to talk with God...

Prayer moves God, and when God moves in your life, things get exciting! Years ago I never dreamed that God would move in my life the way He has. Even after my accident, when I signed up at the University of Maryland for art and English classes, I never realized how God would use diverse elements in my life to mold me to His will. But I sensed God was preparing me for something, and He started me out on a spiritual journey of prayer and praise that has not yet ended. You, too, have a journey through life ahead. Why not make it a journey of prayer and praise? God is in the mountain-moving business! He knows exactly what to do to remove any and every "mountain" that comes our way. "*And when they were come to the multitude, there came to Him a certain man, kneeling down to Him, and saying, Lord, have mercy on my son: for he is lunatic, and sore vexed: for ofttimes he falleth into the fire, and oft into the water. And I brought him to Thy disciples, and they could not cure him.* "Then

Jesus answered and said, O faithless and perverse generation, how long shall I suffer you? Bring him hither to Me. And Jesus rebuked the devil; and he departed out of him: and the child was cured from that very hour. "Then came the disciples to Jesus apart and said, Why could not we cast him out? And Jesus said unto them, Because of your unbelief: for verily I say unto you, If ye have faith as a grain of mustard seed, ye shall say unto this mountain, Remove hence to yonder place; and it shall remove; and nothing shall be impossible unto you. Howbeit this kind goeth not out but by prayer and fasting" (Matt. 17:14-21).Often when we face such a circumstance in our lives, rather than looking to God immediately, we complain, and we moan and groan to our friends. We get down in the dumps, we lose our faith, we ask God where He is – while all the time the Scripture says we should bring our mountains to God so that He can move them for us. But even beyond our personal mountains, when I look at our nation today, I see mountains that seem absolutely insurmountable from a human point of view. When we look at these mountains and then at our own resources, we tend to say, "Lord, there's no way for these mountains to be moved." That's correct – as long as we look at ourselves – for it will take a supernatural miracle of God to change what is happening. The most powerful resource we have as God's people is in looking to God in prayer, believing Him to move the mountains that threaten to destroy this nation. Another characteristic of that type of praying is that it comes from a person who is able to feel the burden of the Lord. We've all heard people get up in Sunday school and read off *a little prayer: "Now, Lord, bless our Sunday school, this, that, and the other." What I mean by prayer that feels God's burden is this: when you and I are willing to get quiet enough, long enough for God to share something of the tremendous weight of the burden of His heart with us, then we'll experience prayer that moves mountains. There has to be some weight. There must be something of a burden from God.*

When is it that your praying really gets down to serious business? When somebody's life is at stake? When some tremendous burden is placed upon you and you begin to vicariously feel something of the hurt, and the pain, and the suffering in somebody else's life? Then when you pray you tell God what you want. You quote Him a Scripture. You remind Him of what He promised to do. That's the kind of praying that moves mountains.

Can you imagine Elijah walking up to that altar of sacrifice and saying, "Lord, I want to pray in Jesus' name, or in the prophet's name, and I sure hope You'll take care of this." Nothing would have happened. Elijah, before God, felt the weight of the paganism and the unbelief of Israel. He said, "It's time you began to make a choice. Stop halting between the two."

The problem with Christians in this country today is we don't hold much of a burden for this country. While we see these mountains engulfing us, we run our way with our pleasure, doing the thing we want to do while God looks for Christians who are willing to be quiet and to feel the burden of what God feels.

When you begin to feel what God feels, something will absolutely transform your prayer life. It will no longer be light, little, perfunctory prayers at bedtime, when you spend just two or three minutes with God. It's going to be the kind of prayer that drives you to your knees, prostrate on the floor before God when you plead with Him to do something you are unable to do. I believe the principle is not only applicable to me, but to every believer: God releases His power only when men are willing to get on their knees in humility, submission, surrender, and yieldedness in the will of God, depending in faith upon God's supernatural power. I believe when we can do that, the windows of heaven will open and a tremendous flood of the blessings of God will come upon us.

We have done everything else. You name it and we've done it. We've had crusades, we've tried everything that comes down the track, but there still has not been a time when this generation of Christians fell on their faces before God in desperation – holding the inspiration of the Scriptures in their heart, believing God, clinging to Him until the asking turns to praising. We only have one resource for leveling the mountains that threaten to crush us and it is available to every one of us. That resource is to pray. If we do not pray, my friends – I want to ask you – what shall we do? If you want your circumstances to change or if you want that mountain to move in your life just pray.

INTERCESSORY OF PRAYER

Intercessory prayer is prayer for others. An intercessor is one who takes the place of another or pleads another's case. One study Bible defines intercession as "holy, believing, persevering prayer whereby someone pleads with God on behalf of another or others who desperately need God's intervention."The background for understanding this calling to priestly intercession is found in the Old Testament example of the Levitical priesthood. The priest's responsibility was to stand before and between. He stood before God to minister to Him with sacrifices and offerings. The priests also stood between a righteous God and sinful man bringing them together at the place of the blood sacrifice. The Old Testament Levitical priesthood was passed on from generation to generation through the descendants of the tribe of Levi. "The Melchizedek priesthood" spoken of in this passage, is the "new order" of spiritual priests of whom the Lord Jesus is the High Priest. It is passed on to us through His blood and our spiritual birth as new creatures in Christ. Jesus Christ is our model for intercessory prayer. Jesus stands before God and between Him and sinful man, just as the Old Testament priests did:

For there is one God, and one mediator (intercessor) between God and men, the man Christ Jesus (1 Timothy 2:5). It is Christ who died, and furthermore is also risen, who is even at the right hand of God, who also makes intercession for us (Romans 8:34). Therefore He is also able to save to the uttermost those who come to God through Him, since He always lives to make intercession for them (Hebrews 7:25).
Jesus brings sinful man and a righteous God together at the place of the blood sacrifice for sin. No longer is the blood of animals necessary as it was in the Old Testament. We can now approach God on the basis of the blood of Jesus that was shed on the cross of Calvary for the remission of sins. Because of the blood of Jesus, we can approach God boldly without timidity (Hebrews 4:14-16).

Jesus was an intercessor while He was here on earth. He prayed for those who were sick and possessed by demons. He prayed for His disciples. He even prayed for you and me when He interceded for all those who would believe on Him. Jesus continued His ministry of intercession after His death and resurrection when He returned to Heaven. He now serves as our intercessor in Heaven. In intercessory prayer, we follow the Old Testament priestly function and the New Testament pattern of Jesus - standing before God and between a righteous God and sinful man. In order to be effective standing "between" we must first stand "before" God to develop the intimacy necessary to fulfill this role. Numbers 14 is one of the greatest accounts of intercessory prayer recorded in the Bible. Moses was able to stand between God and sinful man because he had stood "before" Him and had developed intimacy of communication. Numbers 12:8 records that God spoke with Moses as friend to friend and not through visions and dreams as He did with other prophets.

As New Testament believers, we no longer sacrifice animals as in Old Testament times. We stand before the Lord to offer up spiritual sacrifices of praise (Hebrews 13:15) and the sacrifice of our own lives (Romans 12:1). It is on the basis of this intimate relationship with God that we can then stand "between" Him and others, serving as an advocate and intercessor in their behalf.

Peter uses two words to describe this priestly ministry: "Holy" and "royal." Holiness is required to stand before the Lord (Hebrews 12:14). We are able to do this only on the basis of the righteousness of Christ, not our own righteousness. Royalty is descriptive of the kingly authority that is delegated to us as members of the "royal family," so to speak, with legitimate access to the throne room of God.

DRAFT

Courage To Pray

There are many great prayers in the Bible that can be read and studied to help you know how to pray for strength. Though one of the stories mentioned below doesn't contain the text of the prayer the Bible says that they prayed and God heard them.

Do you find yourself in need of courage for situations that come up in your life? Praying and asking God for courage is the first place you should turn.When Jacob was returning to meet Esau after running away several years earlier, he was more than a little scared. He had tricked Esau and fled for his life. As he returned he heard that Esau was looking for him with 400 men at his side. Jacob prayed to God for courage.

Genesis 32:9-12 "And Jacob said, O God of my father Abraham, and God of my father Isaac, the LORD which saidst unto me, Return unto thy country, and to thy kindred, and I will deal well with thee: I am not worthy of the least of all the mercies, and of all the truth, which thou hast shewed unto thy servant; for with my staff I passed over this Jordan; and now I am become two bands. Deliver me, I pray thee, from the hand of my brother, from the hand of Esau: for I fear him, lest he will come and smite me, and the mother with the children. And thou saidst, I will surely do thee good, and make thy seed as the sand of the sea, which cannot be numbered for multitude."

Read more: http://www.whatchristianswanttoknow.com/10-great-prayers-for-courage/#ixzz4kBxBo9nE

Standing in The Need of Prayer

There is an old spiritual, barely sung anymore, that captures the essence of a heart's cry to God. "It's me, it's me, oh Lord, standing in the need of prayer."

Me. What a hard word, sometimes, to say. To admit.

Many people are in need of prayer – and that is certainly at the heart of the mission of FaithPrayers. But at the end of the day, one thing stands out clearly: we all need prayer. And, we all need to pray.

Sometimes those in the helping professions – the nurses, teachers, therapists, etc. – find, at the end of a day of giving to others, that "It's me, O Lord, who is standing in the need of prayer." But not only because they have given so much, which they may have done, but simply because we all do need prayer. It's not only when we have given, or when crisis strikes, that we need prayer. We need great prayer on the day when things are the most right, when things are the best they have ever been. Because we always need both to pray and have others praying for us.

"It's me, O Lord, standing in the need of prayer..." It's an old song, the author unknown. How fitting, but how sad too, somehow, that the author is unknown.

"Not my mother, not my father, not my sister or my brother, not my elder, not my leader, not the preacher, not the sinner... but it's me, oh Lord, standing in the need of prayer." Those others certainly need prayer too, but it's not the point of the song. The point of the song is humility and honesty.

The song is also a version of the prayer of the publican, or tax collector, that Jesus spoke of as recorded in Luke 18:

"To some who were confident of their own righteousness and looked down on everyone else, Jesus told this parable: "Two men went up to the temple to pray, one a Pharisee and the other a tax collector. The Pharisee stood by himself and prayed: 'God, I thank you that I am not like other people–robbers, evildoers, adulterers – or even like this tax collector. I fast twice a week and give a tenth of all I get.' But the tax collector stood at a distance. He would not even look up to heaven, but beat his breast and said, 'God, have mercy on me, a sinner.' I tell you that this man, rather than the other, went home justified before God. For all those who exalt themselves will be humbled, and those who humble themselves will be exalted." (Luke 18: 9-14).

Standing in the need... there is an enormous difference between being a needy person, as we sometimes use that term today, and about positioning ourselves in a place that we know is honest and accurate before God. It's about owning a truth.

Standing in the need... an old term, not really used today. Searches on the internet or in books are to a large extent fruitless and mainly consist of various renditions of the question, "What does that even mean – to stand in the need?" Does it mean that the singer is in need of others to pray for him or her? Or does it mean that the singer is realizing that he or she personally is in need of spending more time in prayer? Does it mean to recognize a need where one was previously blind to it?

But the writer of the song knew, and the generations past who sang the spiritual knew. And I find it strikes my heart with more power than almost any word that either academics, psychologists, or theologians have come up with. To stand in the need makes greater sense to me than labels and terms. To just stand in that place where you know you need God, whatever else happens.

Standing in the need of prayer... perhaps an acknowledgment of our utter dependence upon God.

Today, at some point, stop what you are doing, and repeat these words, aloud. Definitely aloud:

"It's me, it's me, oh Lord... standing in the need of prayer."

www.ingramcontent.com/pod-product-compliance
Ingram Content Group UK Ltd.
Pitfield, Milton Keynes, MK11 3LW, UK
UKHW041918190726
13854UKWH00003B/1318

9 781387 056446